Write with Impact

Twelve Basic Concepts

to *Influence* Your Story

Marcy Weydemuller

First Print Edition 2018

Book Design by: Stephanie Shackelford: www.SaRoseDesign.com

Photograph by: Bevin Hunter

ISBN: 978-1727332292

Write with Impact Series

"The growth of the imagination demands windows—windows through which we can look out at the world and windows through which we can look into ourselves." Katherine Paterson

Dedication

To everyone who loves stories.

Author's Note

What exactly does it mean to write with impact? This is a question I found myself asking as a writer and a teacher. Regardless of genre differences, in both fiction and non-fiction, we each find ourselves drawn to certain stories and not interested in others, regardless of the quality of writing.

In fact, to my surprise, I've found that some excellent books left me lukewarm and some less well written stayed with me for years. Why? As I wrote, studied craft books, attended conferences, critiqued with fellow authors, and taught writing classes, I found a thread that resonated.

What exactly does it mean to write with impact? When we go deeper into our stories with heart-to-heart connections and associations, we can write stories that make an impact on our readers.

Write with Impact workshops are a compilation of techniques, exercises, and observations that will give your writing a fresh slant, prompt your creativity, and take your writing to a deeper level.

Sometimes the advice, concepts, and exercises will overlap in different workbooks because a core essential can give a strong foundation, which can have different outcomes depending on the intended emphasis.

Whichever workbook you are reading and/or whichever genre is your key focus, I hope you enjoy the journey as you build your own stories.

Write with impact,

Marcy

Table of Contents

Series Introduction

Write with Impact

How can we add a depth to our writing that makes an impact?

Impact=Timeless. When we seed our fiction, and non-fiction narratives, with…

Mystery

Yearning

Truth

Hope

Imagination

Creativity

And then add…

Inspiration

Memory

Potential

Action

Courage

Timelessness

…to our different genres, we connect with ourselves, our story, and our readers. Impact enters into our heart and mind and soul as unforgettable. The concepts and definitions of mythic impact enable us to examine timeless precepts so as to strengthen our stories. And then be able to practically apply them in the nuts and bolts as we write.

When we can make connections to timeless and universal themes, plots, characters and settings, we stir emotional motifs that resonate with readers regardless of genre.

The workshops in this series explore a variety of possibilities to deepen our storytelling to enrich both the process of creating and our reader's enjoyment in the reading. We can merge the myths of the past, the yearnings of the present, and the desires of the future into sighs of recognition. We cross literal and figurative boundaries and barriers that keep us open to new journeys and explorations.

These definitions help lay a writing foundation that is both productive and practical. All the precepts in the series undergird the workshops but often vary in application, such as when they remain as background, and almost invisible, and when they work as a chosen priority.

Introduction

In **Twelve Basic Concepts to *Influence* Your Story** we'll learn how to strengthen our stories by digging deep into concepts and definitions that enable us to examine timeless precepts. When we can make connections to enduring and universal themes, plots, characters, and settings, we stir emotional motifs that resonate with readers regardless of genre. We'll examine tools that enable us to write with impact, read with intent, and watch with insight to nourish seeds of creative exploration and focused imagination.

"Myths are narrative patterns that give significance to our existence." Rollo May

Why do we need myth? What exactly is it?

According to one Google search, myth is defined as:

> *"1. a traditional story, esp. one concerning the early history of a people or explaining some natural or social phenomenon, and typically involving supernatural beings or events.*
>
> *2. a widely held but false belief or idea."*

How to reconcile two seemingly opposite concepts? For example, the Bible itself is filled with stories that fall under the first category and yet there are also a few verses warning against myths as lies.

Rollo May says, "A myth is a way of making sense in a senseless world." Perhaps that is where the crunch comes—what makes sense in one situation can be a serious threat in another and seen as senseless.

Yet when we study myth under the first definition above, we find ourselves building bridges of understanding between a different world and our world. We begin to see with a new perspective. A perspective that drives from a heart-soul story-truth rather than a formal legal rule.

Like wisdom, literature, or love, myths speak across time and across cultures in fresh and ever-changing language. They encompass **m**ystery and **y**earning, **t**ruth and **h**ope, **i**magination, and **c**reativity in myriad possibilities.

Mythic literature refers to stories that have been handed down from generation to generation, orally and finally in print. They include proverbs, parables, wisdom stories, creation, family heritage, cultural, songs, fairy tales, and folktales.

According to Rebecca J. Lukens, the terms "traditional" or "folk literature" express the universality of human wishes and needs. "Folktales have been called the 'spiritual history' of humankind, the 'cement of society,' binding a culture together."

Whether we recognize it or not, myth plays an integral part in our lives. As writers, when we can tap into its qualities we are able to write our stories with deeper impact, regardless of genre. Sometimes myth will drive the entire narrative and sometimes it will add only a few spices. However, its premise of soul language has the capacity to add significance whenever it is used.

An understanding of mythic characteristics can help us see ways to build our stories and write with impact.

Build Your Story: What mythic story has impacted you?

Mythic Definition as Mystery

Albert Einstein said, "When I examine myself and my methods of thought, I come to the conclusion that the gift of fantasy has meant more to me than my talent for absorbing knowledge." Einstein called his imagination "a holy curiosity."

Mythic mystery absorbs this concept of holy curiosity combined with awe.

> "'Manna—what is it?' Israel asked, mystified by the flaky fiber carpeting the earth, surrounding their camp.
> 'Bread from the Lord,' Moses replied. 'Gather as much as each needs, an omer apiece only, one day at a time.'
> They did not, could not, recognize the substance. They struggled to comprehend it, classify it, cook it. Food from heaven. Fare of the angels."
>
> M. Weydemuller

Mythic mystery creates a sense of yearning awe that ignites a heart hunger. It combines a search for answers as well as a willingness to just absorb the beauty and questions left behind.

Science has given us detailed explanations of why the sun rises and sets. Yet the causes do not affect the unique beauty of each one spreading its palette of design across the heavens every day.

Jane Yolen refers to folklore as "constantly transforming and being transformed, putting on chameleon like, the colors of its background." So despite the familiarity, the story is always new and unique.

The lure of a mystery is present in all genres due to the main story question. If we are hooked at the beginning, we will read, even through dull sections, determined to find the end's answer. Chapter and scene endings need to leave us with that pause of "will she or won't she succeed or fail?" The books and movies that keep us wondering breathe that mystery thread with both multiple possibilities and/or multiple questions.

When we add and weave a mythic thread of mystery's awe into our stories, then we can also leave a lingering sense of yearning and a "holy curiosity" that fuels our soul language as well. We write with deeper impact and significance. Like a light breeze causes us to pause, mythic mystery leaves a catch in our throat.

Build Your Story: What aspect of nature continues to fill you with awe?

Mythic Definition as Truth

"Literature proves there is order in the universe. It says that, in life, moral choices lead to outcomes. In fiction there is meaning in human events." James N. Frey

A truth is true or accurate regardless of opinion or debate or rebellion. A truth is true even when information is missing and we cannot readily perceive it. Or have not yet reached a maturity to comprehend its breadth and length and depth and height.

Science, for example, has seen many instances where discoveries and knowledge have opened up previously unbelieved vistas. One major universal fact being that the earth is round, not flat, and that it orbits the sun rather than being the center of the universe. Talk about a complete upheaval of perspective!

Although there continues to be ongoing debate over a "historical" King Arthur, as well as Robin Hood, historians do agree that legends often have a grain of truth in them. And in contrast, a recent television series had one character telling another that, "for a con to work there has to be a grain of truth in it." That true recipe for telling lies goes all the way back to Satan's deceit to Eve over the fruit on the tree.

Mythic characteristics can impact our stories when we tap into the heart truths they represent. Like a parable, there is a surface story and also an undercurrent story that produces an emotional tie.

We make "copies" of the original stories and characters and pass them on through the generations. Some become so familiar that they enter into everyday language as common metaphors, or references, both across languages and within ethnic cultures, giving us shortcuts. Terrible sea incidents become tied to Poseidon allusions, or floods. Rainbows are considered a sign of promise all around the world. Black holes immediately spell danger. So does Godzilla, regardless of the language being spoken.

James N. Frey points out in his book *The Key* that "an astounding example of the similarity of myths from culture to culture is the myth of the hero king."

In Lee Strobel's *The Case For Christ*, he quotes C. S. Lewis: "The story of Christ is simply a true myth: a myth working on us in the same way as others, but with this tremendous difference that it really happened."

What meaning do you want your readers to hear in your story? How might mythic truth help you make that connection?

Build Your Story: What historical or fictional character do you think embodies original heroic attributes?

Mythic Definition as Hope

"For now we see in a mirror dimly, but then face to face…But now abide faith, hope, love, these three; but the greatest of these is love." 1 Corinthians 13:12-13

A mirror reflects images. Outer landscapes often act as mirrors in myth and fantasy, allowing the characters and/or the reader a deeper insight into themselves, a reflection of their inner (soul) landscape, and recognition of shared humanity. When the inner and outer landscapes connect, this combination often illumines spiritual imagery through mirrors and maps. They translate the character's internal landscape for him or her.

In a similar way the mythic stories that are handed down from generation to generation act as mirrors of hope. They include an assortment of proverbs, parables, wisdom stories, creation, family heritage, cultural, songs, fairy tales, and folktales. But a common thread they all share is that the stories are considered of value, the reality of what has gone before and the promises that the future will bring. Through a heart of love they continue to pass along hope.

In some ways myth as hope is tied into myth as yearning although this is not a fabricated put-on-a-happy-face future, but rather an expectation based on experience and relationships and truth. It is hope in story that brings about new beginnings. It shares dreams fitted with solid hiking boots.

James N. Frey, in his book *The Key*, points out that a hero's journey does not necessarily mean the hero will survive, but rather that he succeeds and if he perishes—he dies victorious.

"The hero faces natural fears. They include the terrors of height, fire, wild animals, creepy things, dark places, claustrophobic spaces, physical combat, inhospitable environments, monsters, evil spirits, and perils involving water: storms at sea, rapids and so on." James N Frey

When we can connect our stories to these characteristics and the patterns they provide as they pass down through generations, then we discover and develop personal essence that resonates today. They bridge the past, the present and the future with possibilities—with hope.

Build Your Story: What is the first novel you remember reading that gave you a sense of timeless hope?

Mythic Definition as Imagination

"The imagination is our way into the divine Imagination, permitting us to see wholly—as whole and holy—what we perceive as scattered, as order what we perceive as random." Austin Farrer

Mythic is often considered only as imaginary with the emphasis on made-up impossibilities, or fantastical and unbelievable stories for entertainment. But mythic imagination is actually visionary—a strategy of seeing from a new perspective. It dares to ask the what-if questions to the nth degree. It risks failure over and over again in the attempts to make broken parts whole.

Mythic imagination permeates story and science, exploration and cuisine, language and geography. It is priceless, peerless, and passionate.

It dares to dream beyond the reality it can see and touch and feel. Galileo studied the heavens, improved the telescope, created an early version of a thermometer, and set his world upside-down in arguments by proposing the earth and other planets revolved around the sun. For that he faced a trial for heresy.

Three Persian astronomers, or wise men, followed a star across a thousand miles to welcome a newborn king, born in a stable.

Known primarily for inventing a working lightbulb, Thomas Edison also invented the phonograph and a motion picture camera. With world-changing fantastical consequences. Madam Curie is famous for her studies on radium and Albert Einstein for The Theory of Relativity. He is acknowledged as a genius even though as a teenager he struggled in a school that demanded rote only learning. One of his quotes states, "The important thing is not to stop questioning. Curiosity has its own reason for existing."

Mythic imagination explodes with possibilities. It ignites wonder. It sparks creativity.

Write Your Story: What reality would you like to see re-designed? How would a new perspective change its focus?

Mythic Definition as Creativity

Have you ever noticed how many fairy tales and folktales begin with the concept of a land far away, and yet the "new land" might be just down the road as well as across the horizon? And while following that geography, the tales repeat what would be considered familiar locations: a great forest, across the seas, a castle, a cottage, a road. The people and animals are listed by familiar type as well: beggar, woodcutter, king, peasant, dragon, wolf. Often their immediate actions and choices fall into familiar patterns, but then they have to reassess.

From Aristotle on, many writers believe there are only two basic plot points, which apply to every story. 1) Someone leaves town. 2) A stranger comes to town. Note how perfectly they fit into the land far away mentioned above. And these two stories, as well as other patterns, keep being told over and over.

This is myth as creativity. Regardless of the consistent pattern structure or the basic ingredients, it comes out new and keeps being re-told. Think of Cinderella or David versus Goliath. *Once Upon a Time* has been completely recreated in the popular television series.

Mythic stories look at the familiar surroundings from a different vantage point. What is seen is not necessarily so. It takes a new vision, a deeper look. Whether the journey is long or short in physical distance or in terms of moral choices, the story characters return with a completely new perspective on their old familiar life.

These stories are both personal and universal. No two versions are identical. With each new telling the storyteller brings fresh color and music and conversation designed for this particular audience. It feeds the creative heart much like a child who asks to hear a story over and over again. Which one is your favorite?

Build Your Story: Write your version of the following pattern opening. Turn right at the end of the townsquare and head (north, south, east, west) down the——road. Soon you will see, hear, notice, recognize———Be sure to reach the——by sunset or else you will face——.

Write with Impact Definition: Inspiration

Impact

We've been looking at a *MYTHIC* definition as it applies to storytelling. Now we'll examine the possibilities surrounding *IMPACT* as a definition and how it combines with mythic to deepen its effect.

Inspiration

Memory

Potential

Action

Courage

Timelessness brings mythic elements to life.

Fiction and non-fiction stories need inspiration that is timeless to take root in memories to bring about life-changing possibilities. Why do we read the same book over and over? Or watch a movie countless times? Because something in that particular story at that particular season of our life spoke directly into our hearts.

It may have been a moment of laughter, or an insight into new choices, or a hope that our decisions could bring about a new beginning. Or simply a recognition that it's okay to cry and fail and be forgiven and loved. That good will overcome evil. And that some things in our lives are not under our control. We see relationships build bridges. And that courage can cost everything. In any genre.

Christians around the world celebrate similar faith stories such as Easter. Yet the manner in which Easter is experienced varies widely throughout denominations, languages, and personal family traditions. However, the foundations all are rooted in the same biblical stories. I deliberately used the word stories because although we often refer to the Easter story, it is made up of many parts ending with Jesus' unimaginable gift of grace.

The story begins with Maundy Thursday which includes: The Lord's Supper, a foot washing, betrayal, Jesus' comfort and teaching, including warnings and words about the Holy Spirit, branches, relationships, and prayer. Whew! There is a tension-building novel built into this one night that continues to ripple its applications for every disciple throughout time. Then follows the wrenching Good Friday, followed by a silent grief-stricken Saturday, with Resurrection Sunday, followed by a meal many days later with the same disciples of the Maundy Thursday supper minus one.

Christians know about this story long before knowing this story personally. And they cherish this story no matter how many times it is told. Because, despite all the tears in the telling, they experience inspiration to pick up their lives with a fresh viewpoint.

"All Scripture is inspired by God and profitable for teaching, for reproof, for correction, for training in righteousness; that the man of God may be adequate, equipped for every good work." 2 Timothy 3:16-17 NAS

When our stories are spun, or sprinkled, or saturated, with mythic characteristics, they have the capacity to impact ourselves and our readers with inspirational promise that takes hold in hearts. We can see life with a fresh perspective. Our steps are a little lighter when our words are grounded in truth—even the truth we can't yet see.

Build Your Story: What part of your faith story gives you inspiration for your life?

Write with Impact Definition: Memory

Earlier I asked, "Why do we read the same book over and over? Or watch a movie countless times?" And then I suggested, "Because something in that particular story at that particular season of our life spoke directly into our hearts."

Whenever we participate in a family event or tradition, we carry into the experience all our memories of before. Our personal echoes, whether positive or negative, are attached to us. And they are necessary for our present reality, just as Peter Pan's shadow must be reattached to complete him. Like a parable, there is a surface story and also an undercurrent story that produces an emotional resonance within us every time we remember. These stories help define our desire to continue our family heritage or choose to break away from harmful patterns of behavior.

Family memories are a significant bridge across cultures and generations. Birth, death, education, weddings, parties, and relatives are all common ground even when the actual reality differs widely. Tapping into memories that everyone can identify with adds impact to our writing. We will either bond from similar feelings, or empathize with more compassion the ones that we never imagined.

In the young adult novel *Keeper of the Isis Light* by Monica Hughes, the reader immediately is pulled into Olwen's life as she celebrates her sixteenth birthday, which counts as her tenth on the planet Isis, and at the same time is stricken by the circumstances that she has spent the last ten years as an orphan growing up in solitude with only someone she calls Guardian. Empathy and curiosity pull us into her story even though it is set on a far-off planet. She is real—her emotions are real, her solitude is real. And that impact carries us all the way to the surprising twist at the end of how in fact she survived. Her birthday—a common-ground memory—lays the foundation.

Reading Scripture stories from our diverse heritages gives us a language for our faith journey. And builds in memories for when we might be faced with moral or faith commitments. The memories of how others coped in difficult situations can become path-stones for our own choices as well as for our characters. We may not be called to cross a Red Sea, as did the Israelites, but the courage to take the bridge out of town and begin a new way of living can have a similar exodus journey.

Our past histories can also leave markings on our souls as clear as lines on a paper map. Sometimes they're so worn and smudged we don't recognize their influence, positive or negative, until we come to that corner in the middle of choice. And that is how we want our readers to react when our characters are faced with life-changing decisions.
We squirm and bite our nails, hold our breath, warn them "no don't" or "take a chance" because we relate deep down in our own heart experiences. Using memories honestly helps us write with impact.

Build Your Story: When you were a child, what family story did you want to hear over and over again? Or did not want to hear?

Write with Impact Definition: Courage/Comfort

As writers we are all familiar with the hero's journey, whether we choose to use that concept in our novels or not. And sometimes the criteria for what we first consider to be heroic characteristics can be multi-layered and even opposite.

One of the most interesting assignments I gave my college students was an essay assignment where they compared and contrasted definitions and interpretations of heroes, celebrities, and everyday people. An article on Rosa Parks stated, "Perhaps the most interesting thing about her was how ordinary she was." Almost every essay submitted included this quote. And almost every essay came down to an opinion that courage defined a hero. The courage to act in a difficult situation that might be considered life-threatening, as well as the sheer courageous action of a parent getting up every morning and taking care of the family. Most defined courage as commitment in action.

That perception of courage also became a comfort, because these young college students recognized that, while celebrities might rise and fall, commitment was a choice open to everyone, every day. And that often courage might have been ignored or unappreciated, yet the hero persevered regardless. It gave others hope to face their own difficult circumstances.

Some stories require the celebrated hero, but for impact the core commitment needs to be grounded in everyday reality. There is a trust that this hero would be just as faithful day in and day out. Impact recognizes the courage of an extremely shy character speaking up in a public meeting, or an energetic loud extravert sitting quietly so as not to frighten a young child.

Our stories can resonate more deeply when we recognize and sustain the heart courage in action of our characters, especially the ordinary ones.

Build Your Story: What attributes define your heroes?

Write with Impact Definition: Potential

"The hero is 'separated' from his or her common-day life and leaves to go on the hero's journey: a journey of adventure, discovery, inner growth, and realization that will transform the hero forevermore." James N. Frey in *The Key*

The hero's journey crosses genres and generations, fiction and non-fiction for these same reasons. We pick up a book to read because for a little while we desire to be separated from our everyday world, perhaps have a mini-adventure dreaming of another place to be, or discover a new skill, grasp a new concept that brings us a light into our soul, and step back into our world renewed, refreshed, and with a little more energy.

That is, if the book we've been reading delivers what it promises.

And delivers it truthfully.

The desire for real potential—real fulfillment and emotions—starts young. Almost as if we are already hardwired for a story that has meaning. If you have any doubts borrow a toddler and a stack of books. Watch when his eyes glaze over and he walks away, perhaps making noise to drown out your voice. Or she comes close, climbs into your lap, and almost puts her face in the book in an attempt to inhale it. The book might be written with excellence and beautiful to look at, but if it doesn't capture that child's particular heart it is of no use to that particular reader.

Curiosity and comfort.

Challenge and conflict.

That can be honestly examined and provide a real experience, even when painful, especially in fiction.

For years I felt if I started reading a book, I had to finish it. Now if I reach a point where it is pointless, or repetitive, or absurd, I toss it. There are too many excellent books waiting to be read to waste time on poor quality. Or on a subject for which I have absolutely no interest in pursuing.

As writers, we need to deliver potential that spills over into daydreaming and a sigh when the story ends. A romance where we are clapping for the happy couple, the mystery where we are relieved that justice has been done, the fantasy or sci-fi that opens us up into fresh perspectives, a memoir that bridges communication and understanding with life experiences we would never have, a devotional that honors God and brings us into closer communion. And of course a comedy that lightens our load as we recognize the need to be a little less serious about ourselves and laugh more.

Are you bored to tears writing a particular story? Then chances are you are only skimming the surface and have not dug down deep enough. The journey starts when you can't keep yourself from writing it—*even if no one ever reads it*—because it comes out of your heart first.

Build Your Story: What potential ingredient must be in a novel for you to keep reading?

Write with Impact Definition: Action

"The fiction writer must take responsibility for choosing how the reader will experience the story, because the choices the writer makes will, according to Schorer, be the story's meaning." Jack Hodgins

The cause-effect structure decisions will impact your reader's emotional experience. Hodgins says we are like floor designers who decide what kind of journey it will be. If we push our reader to go to a cosmetic counter via a fish market, or a toy department, he says, we will leave quite different impressions. The writer needs to choose the techniques that will allow the strength of the story to unfold organically—unique to itself.

Do we know who the murderer is from the beginning and watch how the detective brings him to justice, like an Inspector Columbo? Or do we analyze and deduce and ponder along with a Miss Marple? Each style will provide a different perspective both emotionally and mentally. What meaning do we want to linger long after?

The structure choices run throughout each scene. Jordan E. Rosenfeld notes that each scene is to mark an experience and not a lecture. The emphasis of each aspect should reflect the intended design. Intention=impact.

A suspense scene should open with immediate concern for your character. Action scenes need to be quick and intense, driven with a sense of urgency. A dialogue scene carries a main purpose of revealing character, plot, or backstory. Are your characters going to argue, accuse, declare love, plead for forgiveness, or lay down a challenge?

Think of the timeless stories you have known since childhood. What makes them stick? The ebb and flow of drama and stillness? The cadence of the reader or protagonist breathing their fear or purpose into your own heart beating alongside each step they take?

Word choices, atmosphere, tone, and pacing can all be influenced by mythic qualities of significance. Sometimes one word will be sufficient. Sometimes an entire scene, or chapter, needs to be painted with precise brush strokes.

What do you want the reader to experience? What needs to linger long after the final page? Those decisions bring about action with impact.

Build Your Story: What action by a key character in a book or movie have you always remembered? Why?

Write with Impact Definition: Timelessness

"The struggle for human dignity is one of humankind's basic conflicts." Ronald B. Tobias

For any story to have impact, it needs to touch at least one seed of basic needs, kindred spirits, compassion, justice, and many more themes that equal a timeless quality.

Why? That is a basic story question that must be answered every time to have a satisfactory ending. And it is a question each person struggles with personally in varying concerns throughout a lifetime. Throughout eras, and history, and science, and faith.

Tobias says that theme "is your inertial guidance system." However, to have impact, it needs to go deeper than a surface answer, especially ones that may only be plot devices. Even when the subject is a lighthearted comedy or romance, the feelings and questions and answers need to have real substance.

This is one reason I think why some poorly written novels and cheesy movies outvote critical reviews for popularity. Their heart has an essence that resonates in spite of, and maybe because of, many flaws. Readers and viewers identify.

The movie *The Princess Bride* was originally not a box-office success, yet it went on to develop a huge following when released to home video. Many fans can quote the movie almost line-by-line and, according to Wikipedia, a BBC film critic considers it a model to which similar films should aspire.

The *Harry Potter* series upended the publishing world with both positive and negative commentary when it first released. There didn't seem to be any middle ground of opinion when it launched.

From a serious viewpoint, one biblical prophet challenges his listeners with a timeless statement, "He has told you, O man, what is good; And what does the Lord require of you, But to do justice, to love kindness, And to walk humbly with your God?" Micah 6:8

Impact=Timeless. Seed your fiction and non-fiction narratives with mystery, yearning, truth, hope, imagination, and creativity. Then add inspiration, memory, potential, action, and courage as genre appropriate. Impact=heart and mind and soul as unforgettable.

Build Your Story: What does your heart most desire in a story?

Write with Impact

Read with Intent

"A book is a device to ignite the imagination." Alan Bennett

Reading with Intent digs deeper than normal reading and invests in studying the craft to discover the concepts that influence each work. Sometimes you might focus on a particular characteristic and other times examine for a general overview. As you read, keep notes as to what affects you positively and negatively as a reader first. And then dig deeper as a writer.

Reading with intent focuses on discovering quality gems. And identifying sloppy mistakes. Everyone makes some errors, but when the main character in a novel has several different names, that writer needed a copy editor. Or a character changes dramatically in personality with no real reason why is identified. We can then begin to recognize our own weak spots.

For *fiction*, look for main elements and then track the information in a journal. Plot, theme, structure, character, setting, point of view, style, and symbols all work together. One method of reading is to use different color highlighters for different threads. Consider using a cheap secondhand copy so you will feel free to mark it up.

For *non-fiction*, look for target audience, expectations, narrator's voice, attitude toward the subject, world-at-large attitude, overall effect. For example: Hope; what kind? Emotional, physical, spiritual? Solutions: what kind? Cost, time, and/or relational? Entertainment: why? Long term—short term?

Reading with Intent also means reading quality stories in the genre of your choice. In this section we'll look at some wonderful stories by excellent novelists in different categories, as well as quality narrative non-fiction. There's a reason that as readers we become fans. When we find a storyteller we can trust, we always want more.

Historical

On Distant Shores

One of my favorite novelists is Sarah Sundin, author of the Wings of Glory, Wings of the Nightingale, and Waves of Freedom historical trilogies. Yet you don't need to only enjoy historical fiction to appreciate Sundin's works, because her stories capture timeless elements. Her committed accuracy to historical details is the icing. The history weaves seamlessly though lives, as honestly as breathing—simple and complicated together. Her dedication to detail raises the bar, both for the story and for the genre. She makes it look so natural that as a reader you are transported to the common day of her characters.

On Distant Shores by Sarah Sundin is the second of the Nightingale trilogy and a welcome return to the World War II battle zone where the flight nurses struggle for their patients and for themselves.

Lt. Georgiana Taylor loves her job and her life, but as the war continues to batter resources and stamina she begins to wonder if she can genuinely fulfill her role as a flight nurse or if she is in over her head. Especially with her family demanding she return stateside. Then she meets Sgt. John Hutchinson, a noncommissioned pharmacist who challenges her to prayerfully make her own decisions and let God lead her instead.

In return, Georgie's attempts to mend her unraveling circumstances challenge Hutch to live his own words of trust instead of accepting the debilitating misery creeping into his heart as the war erodes his personal life at home and on the battlefields. Even his friendship with Georgie is perilous as rules forbid fraternization.

On Distant Shores catches you by the heart and keeps you reading until the very last sentence. And not want to say goodbye. Just what a well-written novel should do.

Build Your Story: What is the most important concept to you when reading historical novels? How is it different from reading in other genres?

Mysteries

Pacific Coast Justice

Trying to dive into the mystery genre is like trying to decide what to eat at a lavish banquet. The range runs from lighthearted cozy to deep psychological mind games. And even within a category, such as a cozy, the intensity can run from low pulse to heart-pounding marathon.

Within a sub-category, what criteria can be applied to quality, for both writers and readers? Details. I read so many mysteries that it is a pure delight when I find a series that not only keeps me up at night reading but also when I can't wait for the next series by that author.

Inspirational crime novelist Janice Cantore's *Pacific Coast Justice* fulfills both. Main character Carly Edwards is a dedicated police officer in Las Playas, California. She is 'real,' a woman who struggles with relationships, faith questions, and integrity in the workplace. Carly could be our neighbor, friend, or sister.

The shifting clues flow through the plot from the beginning to the end with increasing stress just where they catch a reader by surprise. In addition, as an ex-police officer herself, Cantore brings an added layer of authenticity in procedure and protocol without overpowering the reader with extensive explanations but instead with confidence. That sense of accuracy extends to the locations as well. As readers we see what Carly sees and feels and hears—as an in-the-moment ride-a-long.

Mystery writer Elizabeth George says that the details that show a person's landscape *"imprint an impression of a character in the reader's mind."* The external and internal are achieved through *specific and telling details. These are details with a message attached to them, the kind of details that no reader forgets.* Cantore keeps her characters real and grounded in daily life.

Those specific and telling details are threaded unobtrusively throughout Cantore's series. If you are an aspiring mystery writer, find an author in your specific sub genre who incorporates those telling details, and study the aspects of how thoroughly they are presented. Don't settle on only recent publications but go back and see how the author started off. Or perhaps you need an assortment: one author who describes location well, and another voice, and another plot.

Personally as a reader, I prefer challenge, curiosity, and nail biting without adrenaline terror or graphic sensory overload. I had to stop watching one of my favorite TV series *Bones* when I found myself needing to close my eyes more and more with each episode. However, I recognize my squeamishness is in the minority for that genre. And in reality, it's not a category I am drawn to. The acting and script quality kept me watching even though from the onset I had to close my eyes. Although I consider myself a qualified viewer to assess *Bones,* as a writer I could not possibly pen similar material.

Find the "imprint impression" that impacts you first as a reader, and then write your own quality stories that keep fans asking for more. Enjoy!

In alphabetical order, here are a few more published series that have kept me up past midnight:

Colleen Coble: *Rock Harbor Series* and *The Hope Beach Series*
Earlene Fowler: *Bennie Harper Mystery Series*
Jenn McKinlay: *A Library Lover's Mystery Series*
Ramona Richards: *Jackson's Retreat Series*

Build Your Story: What favorite series have you read recently? What details draw you to read that particular author?

Memoirs

I Could Tell You Stories

"We store in memory only images of value."

Memoir is one of the most poignant forms of storytelling and so akin to a novel that both have been mistaken for each other at times. Reading and studying memoirs offers a banquet of human experience. Where to start? What to recommend? With a bookcase overflowing with excellent memoirs and how to write memoirs, I felt that choosing only one book would be impossible.

Then I realized that whenever anyone asks me about writing a memoir, or in the workshops I teach, this is the first book I hand them—*I Could Tell You Stories* by Patricia Hampl. In this study, the author shares the quality of memoirs by telling stories with rich meaning. It's the perfect place to start craft whether for memoir or fiction writing. Our personal stories within our circle of family and friends will be enriched and our fictional characters more multi-layered.

Hampl notes that memoir is a landscape bordered by memory and imagination. *"For to remember is to make a pledge: to the indelible experience of personal perception, and to history itself."*

As Hampl explores the realm of memory she points out that both Kafka and Rilke saw memory, *"not experience,"* as holding the sovereign position in imagination.

For herself, Hampl discovered: *"The recognition of one's genuine material seems to involve a fall from the phony grace of good intentions and elevated expectations."* What a fresh perspective on motives.

Although she shares specifically via the route of memoir, this door of recognition applies to all forms of writing. If we are unable to infuse our memories into our work, then we rob it of honest quest and discovery and an imagination that connects. Each person's voice is unique and bears witness to life. But in order to share, we first need to identify what really matters to us so we can build our stories, real and imagined, with genuine impact of heart.

"How did I come to believe that what I knew was also what mattered? And, more to the point for the future, is it what matters?"

Build Your Story: What is your favorite memoir? Why?

Classic Corner

The Key

This timeless book is a must-have for anyone who writes fantasy or science fiction. However *The Key* by James N. Frey also addresses core issues that impact all genres, because mythic elements are found at the very heart of all stories that have any impact on a reader.

Mythic features are often considered to be the domain of speculative fiction. But James N. Frey considers them to be the foundation markers for all quality fiction. In *The Key* he sets out the reasons, the functions, the techniques and the possibilities.

One reason Frey gives is that every great fiction story experiences a transformation of character, and mythical journeys and heroes provide universal and ongoing dramatic patterns. We as readers are emotionally and psychologically hotwired to respond. Using mythical motifs increases reader identification and satisfaction in the story.

"If the modern writer is made aware of these forms and the cultural role of myth in the lives of modern man, he or she will be able to use them as a powerful tool that speaks to the reader at the deepest level of the unconscious mind."

To demonstrate, he develops a sample myth-based story. Step by step he introduces the character types, motifs and structures giving clear definitions, and then implements them into the creative draft from idea to outline to rough scenes. And along the way he points out variations and difficulties. This is not a blueprint formula, however.

Frey himself warns against the danger of this trap. *"Nothing could be farther from the truth. The mythic hero needs to be just as three-dimensional, interesting, passionate, and dramatically driven as any other dramatic character. You will need to put more work and care—not less—into the creation of mythologically heroic characters."*

Another important aspect he highlights is subtle perceptions that affect out attitude. He proposes a situation in which his daughter is dating a gas station worker. If he is rude to customers, shortchanges them and is unreliable, then he's a jerk. But if he's employee of the month, courteous and attentive to customer needs, then he's okay. Frey notices that we respect people who are good at what they do, regardless of the job. Recognizing values plays a key insight into mythic heroes in the everyday. Where Frey also adds we find the conflict— in common-day struggles.

Just as his subject stands up to the passage of time, so does Frey's analysis of a myth-based novel in development. Definitely belongs on a writer's classic bookshelf.

Build Your Story: Who do you think is the most complex mythic hero that you have read?

Short Stories

Christmas Excerpts

"I think that finding a voice in writing has everything to do with integrity and little to do with stylistic imitation." Maeve Binchy

As writers first trying to identify voice, and then discovering our own, is often a long difficult road. We often hear editors say they are looking for a fresh voice and sigh, not sure whether we fit or not. Reading through a variety of different and distinct voices helps us to clarify distinctions, which in turn can give us a roadmap to seeing our own so that we can avoid imitation.

When we read through a compilation of short stories by different authors, we will find ourselves automatically drawn to some stories, ambivalent about others, and perhaps even bored by a few, regardless of the quality of writing. This is a valuable method of studying voice because now we ask ourselves some hard questions as a reader. First read a short story for sheer reading enjoyment. Then take a few moments to jot down your initial response. Let it sit for a few days and then re-read with a critical eye. What exactly affected you positively or negatively and why?

Are you bored by the subject itself or the viewpoint? What would you do differently? Is your ambivalence due to the POV character? Why? Do they remind you of someone personally or is their tone of voice off-putting? What would you do to change it? Ask similar questions about the stories you liked—why exactly? What changes if made in that story would cause you to dislike it?

Sometimes it is daunting to dissect a whole novel. Reading a short story collection opens many opportunities to not only examine voice, but also character, scene, theme, language and plot under a welcoming magnifying glass.

Reading in one genre alone helps to narrow a study even more while also showing the wide possiblity of diverse voices. Christmas compilations contain a variety of styles to study. They offer a perfect match for Christmas spirit and meaningful examination.

Three Christmas series I read in the same year offered a wide variety of voices to explore. The series *12 Days of Christmas* by Kathi Macias, told by twelve authors, includes historical and contemorpary stories with both first and third person POV. Both *The Pioneer Christmas Collection* and *The Log Cabin Christmas* have nine different authors.

Build Your Story: What short story collection has helped you study writing? What positive details stood out? Were there any aspects that you considered negative? Why?

Writing a Series

Not only does writing one novel require creativity, stamina, and endurance to reach publishable quality, but writing a series can be like juggling multiple eggs on an ice rink. Just one slip can create a crack that runs throughout the whole series. Often writers don't realize that one novel is about to become a series and have to learn to balance along the way.

Writing the Fiction Series: The Guide for Novels and Novellas by Karen S. Wiesner fills in a long-overdue gap in craft skills for novel writers and it delivers practical advice. Although I knew a preview copy was en route, I couldn't wait so I purchased the Kindle copy to get started. And I stayed up very late my first night reading. This does not happen very often with craft books. In fact, only a few of the writing books I read made it to my column when writing reviews.

Wiesner is also the author of *First Draft in 30 Days, From First Draft to Finished Novel* and *Bring Your Fiction To Life*. One ongoing feature of her books is her inclusion of practical, accessible worksheets and graphs. Organizing one novel can be daunting at times let alone a series. Wiesner blends the organizational skills together into comprehensive sanity.

In *Writing the Fiction Series* she extends her additional resources first, by including ongoing advice and encouragement from series authors and publishers across multiple genres, and second, by making the full interviews available on her website http://www.angelfire.com/stars4/kswiesner/WTSinterviews.html. There are over one hundred. This is a field that is vibrant and hungry for good writing.

And that is the key behind this book: writing a quality series. Wiesner details the definitions, catalysts, styles, focus, organization, and marketing required for any series by showing explicit examples, case studies and stumbling blocks. She thoroughly examines and warns about the importance of characters and consistency when writing across extended novels. On the surface this might seem to be common sense, but in reality it is a danger that can sink your series and lose readers.

I happened to be doing novella research of my own on three separate series in different genres and applied Wiesner's criteria. Some were written by the same author and some by multiple authors. Each book told a good story individually. Every series tripped up. One I tracked for location ties, one for character, and one for premise, an ongoing mystery. The mystery series in particular had all kinds of inconsistencies—the worst being the last book mischaracterized an earlier murder altogether. Not a good way to finish a series and hope readers will return for the next.

Writing the Fiction Series warns you of the potential landmines and shows you navigable routes to write a sustainable high-concept fiction series and enjoy the process. Advice that is long overdue. Advice that is fun to implement.

Build Your Story: Have you ever stopped reading a series you had really liked in the beginning stories? Why?

How To Write Books That Deliver

Writing for Craft Mentor Examples

Every writer has his or her bookshelf favorites. It's important to find the writing mentors who can expand our depth and style in the stories we hunger to write. But there are also some mentors whose writing principles cross over genres and over years. These are the craft books we return to again and again: as beginners, advanced, and professional, because each time we learn something new to apply. They have stood, or will stand, the test of time.

As I read with pleasure a plethora of writing craft books over the years, I keep an ongoing list of suggestions for my students and clients. So if you're looking to add to your own writing library, or give a gift to an upcoming writer, here are some top selections from my favorites.

Getting Started

Writing Fiction For Dummies, by Randy Ingermanson and Peter Economy.

This is one writing book I heartily wish had been written when I started out. Although no time spent on developing craft is ever wasted time, the foundation advice given here enables a new writer to focus on valuable learning techniques, instead of hit-or-miss possibilities.

Crafting Novels & Short Stories, from the Editors of *Writer's Digest*

The editors from *Writer's Digest* have compiled top quality articles from their books and magazines into over thirty-nine chapters to give writers practical applications for craft and creativity. It's a goldmine.

The wide range of talent and perspective offered by the contributors is like a delightful banquet. This book's advice will keep any reader busy for the entire year ahead with pleasurable, propelling instruction. Highly recommend!
The Productive Writer, by Sage Cohen

"The good news is that anything is possible in the realm of productivity if you are clear about the path or goal you are choosing, and committed to discovering and doing what it takes to get you there."

Sage Cohen says that productivity is a lifestyle choice and by the time you finish this book she will cover every aspect of what that lifestyle can look like for a writer. Her suggestions stem from the concept of *"Putting the "You" in Productivity."*

Developing Craft

Make A Scene, by Jordan E. Rosenfeld

Rosenfeld takes basic functions and elements and launches them into powerful scenes. Then she thoroughly examines scene types to highlight their particular qualities and strengths.

The Scene Book, by Sandra Scofield

Scofield doesn't deal only with theory and definitions, but also extends her insights into how-to applications through examples of novels and movies. And then she gives concrete exercises for personal works in progress to find just the right fix to make scenes live beyond correct structure into living scenes.

Showing & Telling, by Laurie Alberts
She cuts through confusion, misunderstanding and error to provide practical understanding towards achieving balance, between showing and telling in both fiction and nonfiction. Alberts gives clear definitions, shows how to use each, in either scene or summary, and how to blend the two together *"to create vibrant and essential prose."* This book is a MUST.

Plot versus Character, by Jeff Gerke

His system integrates plot and character to deepen the quality of your novel, by both building on your strengths and reshaping your weaknesses. However the key dynamic in this book is the detailed development of a character's inner journey. Gerke points out that a good novel can be written without this component and still be enjoyable. Yet, how much richer to experience your protagonist's transformation from the inside out?

The Writer's Compass, by Nancy Ellen Dodd.

Beginning with a story map and a picture map, Nancy Ellen Dodd uses a seven-stage process to combine creative thinking with analytical perspective to shape quality storytelling organically. It is intense. The seven stages are not a formula, but organic, fluid, changeable, and encourage free-form development.

How To Blog A Book, by Nina Amir

Amir covers all the basic how-to questions of blogging in general and how to promote and make a profit. There are three main categories for fiction writers where her suggestions can fortify a writing life with ongoing creativity.
<u>Purpose.</u> Amir's topic questions for characters, setting, genre, and story give guidance towards the reason for the story as well as the needed proposal and promotion plans. Purpose gets you to the heart and enables the portion-by-portion development.
<u>Consistency.</u> The writing becomes continuous and connected. We *finish* the book.
<u>Craft.</u> Composing in bite-size sections on a day-to-day basis highlights the quality we 'publish' next. We tighten our scenes, focus our settings, and build real characters.

Wild Ink, by Victoria Hanley

There are two invaluable reasons to read *Wild Ink*'s second edition. First, it encompasses a thorough introduction to the diverse YA market. Second it demonstrates an excellent understanding of voice from which all writers can adapt her principles to their own audiences. The wide range of possible topics, styles, and content Hanley supplies are also demonstrated by the interviews she includes from several YA authors in fiction and nonfiction. I found it interesting that one common thread was the need to be true to the voice of the story.

Hanley gives an outstanding *Your Inner Teen Exercise* to help identify where you have strengths or weaknesses identifying with the emotional range necessary for honest character development, voice, and dialogue. The questions can easily be adapted to other genres to increase understanding of characterization.

Moving Forward

The Art of War for Writers, by James Scott Bell

In this book James Scott Bell applies Sun Tzu's principles for clarity in battle planning to encourage quality, craftsmanship and courage to writers. He offers a plethora of tactical principles to help each writer along the working path, to harness the courage and skill required to keep writing and reach Sun Tzu's standard.

The Constant Art of Being a Writer, by N.M. Kelby

In her first section, *The Life*, Kelby addresses the basic mindset requirements, decisions, and pitfalls available to all writers. *The Work*, comes next with articles and follow-up exercises on craft skills and how to shape your vision.

In section three, *The Business*, she gives practical detailed advice over what you can control and what you can't: professional conduct, contracts, agents and editors, marketing, book sales, book tours, survival tips and estate planning. Her foundational advice, *"Don't ever lose sight of the fact that you are a writer."*

Marketing

The Tricked-out Toolbox, by Melissa Bourbon and Tonya Kappes

They share as writer to writer and their advice is plentiful: marketing, branding, websites, blog/grog, networking, promotion, trailers, swags, budgets, and PR. One of their best offerings is not in the table of contents but runs throughout the book—sanity.

Classic

Write Away, by Elizabeth George

Novelist Elizabeth George brings the depth of excellence and longevity to *Write Away* that she also does to her absorbing suspense novels. Her premise is that an understanding and mastery of craft will enable writers to navigate the problems we encounter in our novels.

In addition, with each chapter opening she shares an excerpt from her personal journals. These excerpts open a window into the emotional journey that writing requires, regardless of experience and success. Her psychological and practical insights into characterization provide ample creative fuel, regardless of genre.

Build Your Story: What is one of your must-have writing books on your bookshelf?

Journals, Diaries, and Letters

(Perspective)

"…When we have no thought of achievement, no thought of self, we are true beginners. Then we can really learn something. The beginner's mind is the mind of compassion. When our mind is compassionate, it is boundless." Henri Nouwen, *The Genesee Diary*

All writers are well aware of the treasure that can be found during research with journals and diaries and letters, especially for memoir and historical genres. But this area of reading offers gems that can impact all our work. Regardless of our particular field, reading journals, diaries, and letters can give us perspective, expertise, and courage. We'll dig a little deeper into applications over the next few sections.

First: *Perspective.*

Henri Nouwen is a writer who often challenges me in his books, causing me to wrestle with my beliefs and choices, solitude and service. Yet it is in his personal diaries that I am more ready to listen without argument or questions. Why? Because in some ways reading his diary or letters is a form of eavesdropping that is restorative. He shares his heart. And builds a bridge of communication. His feelings are true to him and cannot be dismissed because I don't happen to understand them.

Not only am I neither a man, nor a monk, nor have I experienced hardly any lifestyle close to Nouwen's, but I still have this opportunity to understand him by these very personal writings. And then when I need to write a scene that may involve a person close to one of Nouwen's experiences, I will have some honest thoughts to guide me.

How, as a nonlinear processor, can I possibly write through the viewpoint of a character who cannot conceive of anything other than step-by-step deduction? Or someone in a social or economic strata completely foreign to me, without inserting possible pre-conceived and possibly false attitudes?

Reading private thoughts gives a clearer perspective heart-to-heart that helps bypass arguments and stereotypes. It works for the characters we love and the ones we'd rather never meet. But by grounding them from real live personalities we can write them with more honesty and help our characters grapple with real-life situations. With compassion.

Build Your Story: Whose journal have you read that gave you insight?

(Expertise)

Sea of Cortez by John Steinbeck is described as *"one of those rare books that are all things to all readers. Actually the record of a brief collecting expedition in the lonely Gulf of California, it will be science to the scientist, philosophy to the philosopher, and to the average man an adventure in living and thinking."*

Recently I read a short story Western set in the early 1900s. One character took ill and the other took over the daily diary log for a week, as requested by their employer, and almost went mad with the boredom. As a reader I was on the borderline of skimming any more diary entries myself when the author returned to the main diary person who realized that the reason they were so far behind schedule was due to the enormous amount of time needed daily to keep their nomad livestock alive and healthy. The diary details were short, meticulous and repetitive. Like the record keeping of the *Sea of Cortez* log there was an authenticity to the lifestyle and the work that made the fictional story read like a memoir.

Hopefully as writers we will not cut as close to the edge of boring readers, but to understand and use accurately use details of a job or location or project, diaries and letters and journals written by hands-on participants will give us the verity of expertise. We can see through their eyes and recognize what aspects are important and which are not.

They will also bridge the gap between instructional information, such as reading a recipe, and the emotional response of a working process, such as the texture and smell and satisfactions of kneading dough into bread, or shaping pottery on wheel, or hearing an engine hum after changing plugs and draining oil.

Build Your Story: What diaries have you read that made you feel as if you were present?

(Courage)

"This is the moment when faith is called for. Faith in the creative spirit within me, which is part of what I've been given by God; faith in the process; faith in my intelligence and my imagination. ......I suit up and show up. I sit down at the computer and I do the work, moving it forward a sentence at a time, which is ultimately the only way there is to write a book." Elizabeth George, *Journal of a Novel, July 6, 1998.*

Reading a collection of letters gathered over a period of time gives an extremely personal inside view of why the writer continues to keep on going through many trials and how they live out their worldview perspective. Which in turn can give readers, or characters, some insight as to how to apply or reject a viewpoint by seeing the long-term influence emotionally and psychologically.

Even when some of the letters are written with the intent to be read for public consumption, there is still a key purpose or concern being offered. The apostle Paul knew his letters would be circulated among many churches. People who write letters to the editor or an organization consistently have a message they want heard. Elizabeth George wrote her letters about her novels to herself.

C.S. Lewis wrote many letters for publication and literary intent, but he also wrote to a woman he never met without expecting his letters to be made public. His *Letters to an American Woman* included discussions and encouragement and personal sharing.

Family letters become even more personal, either from one to another emptying their hearts, or conversely, protecting their loved ones from knowing what they are going through—each poignant from a different angle.

Need your own brand of courage to face a personal or vocational issue? Look for letters and let another's journey walk alongside you or your character.

Build Your Story: Do you have a special blog (modern-day version of letters sometimes) you go to for inspiration? What does it offer to make you keep reading?

A Heart for Inspirational Romance

Quality inspirational romance requires the same credentials as all romance novels: real characters, strong plots, relentless conflict, scenic settings, and love's heartbeat at the center. These characteristics are expected regardless of subgenre or topic, which also mirror other romance subgenres. Contrary to some misconceptions, there are almost no forbidden topics in inspirational romance. Life deals out harsh realities regardless of background or culture. Broken relationships, strained finances, violence, disease, and lost dreams walk side-by-side with new beginnings, birth, celebrations, and fresh opportunity. The main difference in this genre is the "life-scape" lens that filters choices.

In addition, there are three extra attributes to inspirational romance that draw and maintain loyal readers: fellowship, insight, and hope.

Fellowship. When any reader picks up their favorite genre, they expect a certain return for their time. A cozy mystery reader does not expect a grisly, psychological thriller. Inspirational readers turn to long-standing authors such as Janet Oke, Francine Rivers, or Lauraine Snelling because they expect to spend an afternoon or evening with a trusted friend who will deliver the particular uplift or challenge they need. It's the one-on-one version of going to the local café to offload some emotional shake-up with friends. When you leave the café or the book, you feel soul-stronger, ready to take up whatever your next step might be. The fellowship binds readers and authors because it's built on trust. They know from experience these friends will deliver. Then they'll look for other writers who write in a similar vein as their main friend, thus expanding the circle. What kind of fellowship do you want your character to offer your readers?

Build Your Story: Begin brainstorming your character's heart.

1. What is her go-to choice of movie, book, music, or food when she needs comfort or courage?
2. Whom has she trusted the most with her heart's desires, past or present, alive or deceased? Why?

3.   Where is she most discouraged right now? What would give her hope?

Insight. Whether flying the skies over Europe in the historical World War II series Wings of Glory by Sarah Sundin, or time traveling in Italy with Lisa T. Bergren's River of Time series, inspirational romance gives insight, clarity, and discernment, by modeling real lives struggling with real relationships. All without telling or teaching or trampling.

We may not be the ace pilot with a slightly enlarged ego, but we might recognize that the words his friend had been quietly speaking are similar to the ones our trusted friend has been speaking to us. And avoid the fall-out in our own relationship because we listen. Or find the courage to confess an indiscretion and trust it will lead to reconciliation. Outer circumstances change along a timeline, but hearts don't. Struggles over envy or greed or fear remain. Desire for love, acceptance, and understanding never end. Good fiction mirrors heart-life and in inspirational romance readers can trust the foundation.

Hope. Inspirational romance springs from a faith-based perspective. Often when we really need personal advice we go to someone who not only has known our ups and downs but also has stayed by our side through them. They already speak our heart and soul language. We have confidence to know we are using the same vocabulary.

Author Gail Gaymer Martin notes that there are three threads in inspirational romance: personal, romantic, and spiritual growth. As the characters grow into their relationship with each other, they also develop a relationship with God in their individual faith walk. Understanding and developing their spiritual needs sometimes will draw them closer together and at other times will drive them further away. However, the end result will always be hope, even if it is only a sliver of light.

Inspirational romance is heart romance inside and out—changing lives, restoring souls, and creating new beginnings, all grounded in love.

Build Your Story: What authors do you know who share all three aspects in their romances?

Watch With Insight

"Scenes are the building blocks of fiction," James Scott Bell.

Like the roads we literally travel on, we continually need to view our writing to understand where we are and to make sure we haven't gotten lost. What does that sign say: danger ahead, construction work in progress, slow down, curve, slippery, speed limit? The story route is as much a part of the journey as the destination.

Mythic motifs, often identified through the imagery of mirrors, and maps, echoes and allusions, connect us to their timelessness. When employed naturally, they provide a deepened resonance. Their rich history can be mined for today's stories because the emotional truths of a new perspective, story, courage, hope, possibilities, mystery, metaphors, and symbols still apply.

Metaphors build bridges of fresh 'soul' language, *maps* give possible direction and connections between external geography and "internal" landscapes. *Memories* offer echoes, and seeds of *mystery* create curiosity and knowledge. Their timeless elements can add an extra layer of depth to any novel across genres.

Movie deconstruction provides novelists another way to study scenes and motifs in small segments. Just as beginning artists often copy master painters in the galleries to hone their skills, studying or "reading" movies gives us a visual angle to examine.

Mythic elements have contributed to the success of many movies such as *Star Wars, The Princess Bride, O Brother, Where Art Thou, Troy,* and *Raiders of the Lost Ark.* In this section we'll look at some movie examples of resonance through the lenses of metaphors, maps, memory, and mystery.

Each movie is divided into the four categories so that you can choose whichever concept you would like to study and make a few choices of movies to compare according to the difference in genre focus or mythic motif or both.

Whichever movie you choose, either from the examples or some of your own, I suggest that you skip the preview opening and scene selection headers, and turn off the sound for the first time you watch the opening scene. Make your observation notes then re-watch with the sound and consider any differences you notice. In what ways does the musical atmosphere set up an emotional background?

Phantom of the Opera

Metaphor

Visual metaphors often speak in silence. Their images impact emotionally and mentally. All our senses are engaged. Movie opening screenshots can communicate volumes of possibilities within a few minutes by tapping into our universal feelings and engaging our curiosity. And yet while all audiences see the same imagery, we often process the material individually.

Sometimes it's hard to get past all the introductory fanfare, but when we can observe up close, as in a freeze-frame, the metaphors explode. In a recent workshop students shared their observations on the opening scene in *Phantom of the Opera*, which is shot in black-and-white. While we all related to the ambiance and noticed the same details, each one found one or two images that held a primary impact.

For example, the ruins of the opera house were coated with cobwebs. Seems to be a natural connection, but as one student pointed out the cobwebs, it took on a deeper meaning. Just as a cobweb is a concentrated and patient work of art, so was the Phantom's training of Christine's voice. Just as the cobweb is a lure for a spider's meal, so was the lure to Christine to join the Phantom in his world. And also as the cobwebs clung to the fixtures after decades of decay, so did the Phantom's story cling to the frail elderly visitors to the auction.

Build Your Story:

1. Look over your beginning scenes. What common natural images do you have in your setting? Make a list of them and then next to each one write a possible emotional metaphor. Choose one that can be threaded unconsciously throughout the novel.
2. Develop its characteristics so you will have the details ready when an opportunity opens to include them.

Maps

Emotional maps are unique, even from within a shared experience. Have you ever reminisced over a family incident or vacation, and been astonished at the different highlight memories? The geographical location was identical, but the perspective diverse. Or discussed a memory that to you is almost as vivid as the day it occurred, but another family member shrugs with no recollection at all?

The opening scene in *Phantom of the Opera* sets up a common ground physical map of emotional experience, first present and then past. It is a bleak day. The access route to the opera house is cold, wet, and icy. The elderly need assistance. And once inside the interior proves even more hazardous. There is no shortage of concrete physical metaphors in the decayed building. One student in the discussion remarked, "I saw it also as the future being the death of the past."

Upon arrival the elderly bidders nod to each other with respect. In that moment they acknowledge their common ground for being present to this auction. And then both choose to bid on the same item. Ignoring what to the outsider might be considered art works or antiques when presented, they focus on a battered, tarnished child's common toy, a monkey that plays cymbals.

Both want it and keep raising the bid for the seemingly worthless item. And then they pause to look at each other. Sorrow etches their faces. And the woman acquiesces, as she recognizes in him a deeper need, an emotional map that needs closure.

Build Your Story:

1. Take a humorous circumstance that your character has experienced, and retell it from the future looking back at least forty years. What stands out in vivid recall?
2. Repeat, but now use an emotionally difficult decision.

Memory

Memories are often like torn spiderwebs. You follow the thin thread a little unsteadily and then suddenly there's an open space. What's missing? You look down to the next tier of strands, or perhaps up, hoping for a closed portion, but the ends straggle in the emptiness.

It's a muddle, like an early morning gray fog that shifts around you in swirls.

Phantom of the Opera's opening scenes, shot in black-and-white, give the same sense of movement, as different objects fade in and out of highlight with different degrees of shadow. Why is it important to remember that particular item? As the camera light passes over each object, it further shades them like a passage of time. One student commented that, "there are shades of gray in all of life's stages."

So when we look back into memory, to gauge our progress or to find a foothold for the future, sometimes uncertainty hangs in wisps like the spiderweb. And then a slight flush of air pushes another strand into view—just over there—just near the empty space. Now comes the decision. To jump, or not? And suddenly the image is blazing with color.

Build Your Story:

1. Choose a turning-point memory in your own life, or for your character. Write it up with as many details as possible. Don't worry about overwriting it. Pour in sensory specifics.
2. Now color code the sensory highlights as if you were filling in a stained glass window or a paint-by-number. Which color is predominant?
3. Now re-write as a scene capturing that particular focus.

Mystery

To unravel a mystery involves many choices, decisions, and persistent questions. But to unravel a historical one requires another set of problems regarding where even to begin. How to know what elements are important enough to pursue?

Phantom's opening scene is shadowed with possibilities, all coated in shades of gray. All the viewer has to lean toward is the two interested bidders, so seemingly out of place in the opera house mausoleum. Yet they must be there for a reason. They have obviously chosen to attend this auction despite adverse conditions.

When the elderly man and woman vie for the same item, they repeat their initial respectful nod. Yet they still choose to bid against one another. So the mystery is not between them as a relationship, but is held somewhere within their mutual desire for the musical toy, a commonplace item.

It is such a deliberate purposeful action that makes clear a choice will be a major theme in the story about to unfold. The atmosphere of the first scene is ominous, one student noted, but it does not *"yet have the measure of how choices effects the characters."* Only a beginning hint, resting in a child's battered toy.

Build Your Story:

1. Make a list of old-fashioned toys such as the ones that every generation has enjoyed. For example action figures have longevity, even though once they were regimental tin soldiers and now they may be space aliens.
2. Choose the least likely from your list and place it in your antagonist's room or suitcase or deluxe office. How incongruous is it to an acquaintance? What questions does he wish he could ask?

Green Dragon

Metaphor

When a character is in an unfamiliar external or internal environment, familiar creative pursuits such as gardening, cooking, music, or art can become mirrors, reflecting a spiritual alliance to another place. They can translate the characters' soul landscape into some sense of stability as they respond to these metaphors. Sometimes these responses come in action, sometimes in desire or longing, sometimes in a symbol. These images often find a voice within the small common-ground creativity built into everyday activities.

The movie *Green Dragon* has an abundance of metaphoric symbols that on the surface are not at first recognized as connected. For one, the commanding staff sergeant takes photographs throughout the camp. He thinks he is doing so to keep a record of the historical circumstances and of the people who have been impacted. But it is through the photos and their images that he himself comes to terms with his own secrets and need for healing.

And in another small action, an elderly refugee general plants a seed. An orphaned refugee boy, Minh, watches intently as the old man daily waters a tiny dirt patch. Minh tries to understand why he is even trying to grow anything in the makeshift camp. But like a living photograph Minh is drawn to watch the daily routine. And when the old man dies Minh takes his place, watering and waiting to see what exactly lies under the ground. The general had lost his "voice" to give to his people, and turned instead to nourish a new symbol of hope. When Minh presented the first offering from the tiny growth it shook the camp.

Build Your Story:

1. Choose two different movies from your personal favorites and watch the immediate opening of each with the sound on mute. What images stand out?
2. Re-watch with sound. What changes—if anything?
3. Apply to an ongoing activity for your character. What are some repetitive common actions? Make an image list for them.

4. Choose details that turn them into metaphoric symbols.

Maps

What happens when the "map" of existence as you know it disappears? Instead of a broad landscape, you have only a tiny space allotted to you. What will shape your new reality, emotionally and geographically? Going camping in nature gives us a taste of adventure, but fleeing your home with a few grabbed possessions sets a different tone to the journey.

In the movie *Green Dragon*, many find solace in establishing daily routines. One young woman volunteers at the sewing tent, and a young entrepreneur tries to set up a mail order business—to help ease the circumstances and to learn to adapt to this new "land" as he is anxious to move forward as soon as possible. Others try to settle in this new location and physically resist leaving the camp when the opportunity arises to find an outside sponsor family. Even with nothing left but a cot in a corner, they still are among their culture and language and refuse to be separated from the threads they still have.

The young children map out their new surroundings and then make a daily tour. Minh in particular makes sure he watches the old man watering his patch of dirt and visits the cook to watch him paint. He diligently reads the notice board, watching for any hint of his family, takes a stand at the arrival gate, checks the bathhouse, the eating tent, and the women washing clothes. He comes to know the routine and lives the camp inside out. When the time comes to leave, his understanding and adaptation to new territory becomes the bridge across his uncle's fears.

Build Your Story:

Put your character in a situation where she either dreams, or actually experiences, a "refugee" relocation. It can be either by war or natural disaster. What is the first thing she does to give her space a personal focus? Or how does she resist?

Memory

Shared memories can open up windows into broad horizons. Even when the memories are painful or contradictory, the willingness to talk about them creates a space for wholeness. Or at least a different perspective. If left unspoken, hurtful scenes may board up bitterness and destruction closing off any fresh air.

The movie *Green Dragon* depicts the story of Vietnamese refugees after the fall of Saigon. Crowded into army tents and Quonset huts, the assortment of survivors cover a broad spectrum: young and old, civilian and army, educated professionals and laborers. And across that divide are religious, political, and economic strata, now all together experiencing a common grief from their individual sorrow. In the movie there is at first a stoic silence, even within a family unit. No one is willing to share. Bit by bit the numbness eases. One day a man takes out his instrument and begins to sing a national song, and the camp quiets into listening and then gradually adds their voices and their tears.

This common ground, experienced through a beloved song, drew them together in memory. And as they began to share with each other their escapes, their fears, their losses, they took steps toward a new horizon.

Build Your Story:

1. Choose a situation for your character with a sibling or friend where they have opposite emotional memories, one positive and one negative.
2. Write up a page of dialogue between them as they remember it.

Mystery

Change, no matter how small, can create mental and emotional chaos as you turn in a different direction, physically or emotionally. To cross a threshold though requires a choice, even if it has been forced upon you like a refugee fleeing his war-torn land. All sensory memory is heightened and sharpened. It is not just the moment that is at stake, but the journey that follows it. Thresholds become part of our soul shadows as much as our physical bodies cast their shadows. And the question can linger. "Did I choose the right fork in the road?"

In the movie *Green Dragon*, Tai is forced to make a deliberate choice for himself and his newly melded family as a threshold crossing into a fresh beginning. He must face a country filled with mystery, compared to the one he left behind and probably will never return to.

On the surface it is a passage of a moment. Yet it includes walking away from a place and choosing to no longer be who he was a few minutes earlier. At first, fear paralyzes him from taking that step into discovery. There have been too many changes, too many losses and disappointments. Then his American friend takes him for a drive over the dried-up hills to investigate the small town just beyond the camp walls, just beyond sight. And he returns with a grocery bag filled with familiar foods. He returns beaming with possibility and encouragement, not only for himself but also for the other refugees. A new possibility has bridged the gulf of despair into hope. He is ready now to face mystery with anticipation and curiosity.

Build Your Story:

1. Choose a psychological threshold that your character must face at each main stage of the novel structure categories: set-up, response, attack, and resolution.
2. Which one has the most emotional impact? Write it up as a new scene.

The Secret of Moonacre

Metaphors

Peering into one metaphor alone is like looking though a prism of possibilities. A well-chosen and well-placed phrase provides a dazzling vista of interpretation. For example, a recent conversation on "a castle" included multiple ways to focus a setting through metaphor and theme.

In the movie *The Secret of Moonacre*, there are two distinct castles, each a reflection on choices. The choices were made hundreds of years earlier but continue to enslave the descendants as each generation takes up a personal decision to perpetuate the feud.

One castle is in ruins—empty, cold, a shadow of its former life. It is a place of sorrow and lost opportunity with only three inhabitants left.

The other castle is stark, cold, grey, and brimming with people. Busy, bustling, inhabitants filled to the brim with anger and revenge. And a closer look reveals a castle in decay as well.

Both castles have become mirror images of heart choices. The reality of this concrete metaphor unfolds with greater perception as the story shows all its secrets and mysteries.

Build Your Story:

Choose the place that is most important to your character or most central to the story question. Costume it from a variety of styles: old and decaying, ordinary, flashy, sophisticated, copycat, or with a brand-new coat of paint. Which version becomes a metaphor for your character's heart?

Maps

Information boards and kiosks, from local hiking trails to prestigious museums, have one common note: "You are here." The maps may be plain, in color, different sizes, with or without words, but the X marks the spot is clear enough to give the visitor a sense of place, a center from which to choose their direction.

Not only do these information markers cut down on employees being asked to give directions, but they also add a sense of safety and security emotionally. Disorientation in physical surrounding often results in immediate stress. For adventurers it's an adrenaline rush of excitement, but for others it can raise fearful memories. Either way we prefer to have some measure of control.

In the movie *Moonacre*, orphan Maria Merryweather is introduced to her new country home as her uncle takes her for a ride around the land, marking out the boundaries, and giving clear warnings as to where she should not go. But he also refuses any explanations, both for external dangers and her internal confusion. He removes her father's book despite her pleadings and locks it away in a forbidden room. He tells her what she may and may not do, and then ignores her questions, often dismissing her with curt exits.

Left with only a partial map of her new surroundings, she attempts to find some solid ground emotionally and tumbles into more and more bewildering situations. Still she tries to make sense of where she is, and why her uncle lives as he does, and what does it all have to do with the hidden book.

Bit by bit she explores this new territory and creates her own map to discover what her inheritance really is.

Build Your Story:

Take your character to the home of a relative she never knew existed. Literally or figuratively, close the door behind her. How does she get her bearings in this place? What emotional roller coaster does it unleash?

Memory

Busyness, stress, aging, and noise are just some barriers that affect our day-to-day memory retention. Time slips away and we realize we've forgotten an errand, or a phone call, or to pay a bill. So we cope with various methods to help us remember, but we also don't let the frustration control us.

Long-term memories, however, have the capacity to cripple plans and relationships when they become so entwined in our minds and hearts that we measure all our decisions against them. Especially when our memory has become distorted over time. Like the telephone game children play, the whispered word or phrase at the end is completely different than the beginning, and usually unintelligible.

In the movie *The Secret of Moonacre*, memories of an event are passed down from generation to generation, each adapting it to their own perspective. The meaning behind the original event is completely submerged under suspicion and accusation.

Each side of the conflict fuels the animosity, all built on a faulty foundation. When newly arrived Maria Merryweather comes to live in this environment, she realizes that if the truth isn't discovered there can be no restoration. She begins a search through all the stories and memories trying to find the true thread. Her fresh insight finally breaks down the twisted memory brambles and releases everyone to start fresh.

Build Your Story:

Take a special event from your past and write it up as a free-write, not pausing, just pour out all the pieces you think you remember. Then write down all the emotions that still influence you from that memory.

Ask a sibling or friend or family member, who was also present, to share their recollections. How close are you emotionally? What different details stand out?

Apply this idea to one of your characters. Have them completely misunderstand an event and make decisions based on that faulty impression.

Mystery

Curiosity begins before it has language to express itself. Watch an infant seeing his environment or a toddler discovering a ladybug. Then as language expands the questions come buzzing incessantly for answers. Where are we going? How does it work? What makes the sky blue? Why?

Spending a few hours with a mystery novel or movie refreshes us and feeds our natural curiosity. Not only do we take a break from our normal schedules, but also we can exercise our imagination and our deductive reasoning together. An enthralling mystery nurtures all our senses.

Often we only need a title to draw us in. The movie caption, as in *The Secret of Moonacre*, tells us what we are to discover. Or does it? What is the secret? The answer is quite simple but the path to it is long, with twists and turns emotionally and physically. It is covered over by layers of misinformation and misunderstandings.

Why did her father leave her only a battered old book? Why can she see the story when she opens it? Why does her uncle lock it away from her and refuse her access?
Why is everyone so angry? The questions swarm like bees. One answer opens another and then another until she is running to escape the onslaught. And yet she must find the answer now for herself. Her curiosity pulls her deeper and deeper.

Build Your Story:

A few weeks after an elderly relative has died, your character receives a special delivery envelope. Inside is a key, a locket, a note from her relative that says, "I'm sorry," and an oilskin pouch containing a map of his summer home and a fragile ink-smeared letter that is at least fifty or more years old. What happens next?

Avatar

Metaphors

Metaphors also incorporate juxtaposition to catch our wonder. The movie *Avatar* brims with metaphors, creating not only a visual panorama, but also a breathtaking palette of concepts.

The floating mountains startle us. Our perspective struggles to grasp our familiar assumptions of weighted solid rock suddenly floating in transparent air. We need mountains to stand firmly on the ground, don't we? So we can admire their grandeur, scale their heights and conquer the elements. All are still possible in *Avatar*'s world, except that if anyone falls, they fall into air. Both the beauty and the danger are heightened to an unimaginable level.

Sometimes we become so familiar with the language and images we use in our writing that we sap their strength. We know to avoid clichés, but often we settle for ordinary when with a metaphoric dab we might shatter open new possibilities.

What about some rock-hard assumption we make for our characters or ourselves, positive and negative? What could happen if we released them into air? What consequences could follow?

Build Your Story:

1. Make a list of natural elements that we expect to be free-floating. Now ground them as with the weight of a mountain. What new concepts do they provide?
2. Repeat using personality traits in yourself or someone you know well. Then apply the change to one of your characters.

Maps

Ancient travelers observed nature to guide them to their destination. They depended on the position of the sun, moon, and stars as reference points. They tracked the wind. They examined ground and foliage to trace water sources.

Today we have computerized maps and guidance systems to talk us through strange surroundings, or we can send quick text messages to ask others who know.

Avatar's world unfolds one view of technology overload. The military is completely dependent on their machines for breathing livable air, industry, protection, and travel. Without their machinery they are virtually helpless on this strange planet. And yet they see themselves as conquerors, as an advanced people, who openly disdain the native population.

But they are locked in their steel worlds and are unable to navigate or explore without taking life risks. They pre-set their radius maps, emotionally and physically, and stay hostage in a false sense of safety. They follow programmed sight. Until they reach the floating mountains with magnetic force that sends all their instruments askew, and they have to fly by eyesight. Watchful. Careful. Really see the land around them: beauty and danger side by side.

Build Your Story:

Choose a travel destination for your character. Is it familiar territory or new? Will she jump in her car and just go? Or plan every step for every possible emergency. Are her precautions common sense or anxiety ridden? Examine her attitude as she approaches each marker en route and show your reader how she perceives her trip.

Memory

Personal, public, and cultural memory has the potential to loom over current decisions and negotiations in either positive or negative terms. If the memory is old enough to be considered history, it can turn itself into a legend that may or may not have any bearing in reality, other than as a name or a place.

And yet we often use these memories as measures against others and ourselves. That is, if we think one is valid. Or, if we consider it as impossible and only vivid imagination, we will make a concerted effort against it. However, the legend may contain truth that unlocks hope.

In the movie *Avatar*, Jake has lost all possibility of negotiating a peace. He has completely lost the trust of the people he now loves. Desperate for a solution, he remembers the story of the Toruk, the mighty predator of the skies, caught by a leader at times when the people were in danger. The previous Toruk riders brought them victory, so Jake sets out to become one, not knowing whether the legend was real history or story, or a mix of both. But it is enough to give him enough courage to try.

Build Your Story:

Under what conditions would your character be willing to turn and trust in a story, or legend, or person that may or may not be true? Under what conditions would you?

Mystery

Often when we encounter a new idea or challenge it excites us. The joy of discovery and the puzzle of understanding with insight grips our imagination. We're eager to share our delight. Our amazement. But then another mystery follows. Others don't find it as interesting, even those closest to us, whether personally or vocationally. Or they're not willing to put in the time and effort necessary to comprehend all the implications.

Perhaps solving the mystery is only a prelude to years of painstaking research with personal risk, as so many doctors and scientists have done to find medical cures.

In the movie *Avatar,* after years of study the scientists make an astounding realization. They realize that the indigenous people connect within their world like a neural network. They have achieved an interconnection between all living organic matter, which is far beyond mankind's achievement.

They rush to stop destruction, desperate to protect the people and the science. But then they face rejection and ridicule, and finally are confined to jail to get them out of the way. This mystery costs them everything. Their breathtaking words split open the wide gulf of difference between values and beliefs.

Build Your Story:

Your character has discovered a truth that can bring healing to mind, soul, or body. How does he communicate that discovery? How does he react when others reject his gift of life?

British Mini-Series

Metaphor

It's interesting how a metaphor can contain a number of meanings, and that even when it has the same meaning it may also carry a variety of perspectives. Over the past year I've watched several period piece series from Britain. *Downton Abbey* and *Lark Rise to Candleford* top the list with the quality of actors and setting. However, all have phrases, metaphors, and references to common historical threads that don't necessarily transfer to other heritages.

For example, the central importance of the manor and all that it implies. "To the manor born" reflects an inheritance to prestige and wealth. It also means a personality is well suited to manor living. But in many circumstances it's not only the titled families that are born and raised into the manor, but also many servants can trace their heritage back decades to a lifestyle bound to the manor.

Tenant families considered a position tied to the estate, or in the manor itself, as the highest possible opportunity for their children. Both segments of the societal hierarchy took their positions and privileges seriously. However, newcomers to the manor often saw it simply as a job and sometimes with disdain. Not all inheritance manor families accepted their position as a responsibility but took it as a right and misused their power.

Using the word *manor*, even literally as a location, has the potential to create emotional tensions, questions, and perspectives. One word alone can open up multiple threads of possibilities.

Build Your Story:

1. Choose an expensive dinner celebration, such as an anniversary or graduation.
2. Choose four people involved in the actual meal and write a few sentences for each showing their feelings. Suggestions: guest of honor, family member attending, a staff person in the restaurant, a server or cook in the kitchen, a passerby, another diner close enough to overhear pieces of conversation.

Maps

One tiny smudge on a map, or a slight error, can be enough to send a traveler miles off their route. The delay may be a minor side trip or a serious delay in destination. An East Coast conference I once attended had to revise two days' worth of lectures and speakers because the airlines had inadvertently sent a main presenter to a Western state in error. They had made an assumption based on the city name and didn't take the time to notice the state address. Then winter conditions aggravated the correction.

Misheard or misunderstood conversation fragments can also send a character down a wrong path. In the BBC series *Downton Abbey*, a servant is chastised for crossing respectful boundaries and, instead of acknowledging her error; she fusses and bears a grudge. Then while eavesdropping, she overhears a snippet of conversation and believes she is to be replaced. From then on, her attitude and actions become increasingly hostile. Finally she acts on her feelings and makes an immoral decision. Even though she immediately regrets it and turns to undo it, she is too late, and a death occurs.

While grieving both her own choices and the loss in the family, she discovers that, rather than replacement, her mistress had been holding her up as an example of a quality lady's maid.

Build Your Story:

1. Make a list of possible comments someone close to your protagonist might say about her actions. Make the range from very negative to glowing support.
2. Have your character overhear a portion of one of those statements. How does she "hear" it emotionally?
3. What is her immediate reaction and her long term reaction to this fragment of conversation?

Memory

Some memories we hold on to with such fondness that they gain a saintly status over time. Likewise, parts of our past we'd rather not be reminded of increase in regret to the point we lock them away. Sometimes we actually forget they exist. Until a memory surfaces as in a jolt and we're forced to acknowledge it.

The very proper and fastidious butler Mr. Carson, in the BBC series *Downton Abbey*, crashes into his past face to-face as an old acquaintance forces his way into Carson's life. This encounter also shows the shifting social atmosphere that this charlatan would actually dare enter the estate, especially by the front door. But he is made bold by Carson's own fears and attempts to keep him quiet from exposing his previous life as an entertainer.

Faithful to "his" family and the position he holds, Carson sees only the possibility of disgrace and loss. In fact, he offers his resignation when all comes to light. Fortunately his employer sees through the blackmail. He also recognizes Carson's longtime service to the family and sets that commitment as more valuable that Carson's previous life. Although mildly amused at the concept of Carson in show business, he does not give the situation the weight of shame that Carson himself has. Now Carson is able to see his own memories with a different perspective and interpretation. And yet, his initial concern would have been completely accurate had the dowager been in charge. She would have immediately dismissed him without even a hearing.

Build Your Story:

1. Make a list of activities your character participated in when young.

2. Choose one that could become an embarrassment for her if revealed in her workplace or at a social function. Make the teller someone who is putting a sinister or shameful twist on her participation.

3. What does she stand to lose if the story is accepted at face value?

Mystery

Have you ever played the character game where you guess what a person's job is based on how they're dressed? With the business industry's more relaxed protocol over the past few years, it's a little harder to gauge apart from a uniform or a logo. The next step is to guess what the duties are in their section of the tier. Society still seems to measure people by position, regardless of vocation. And then find ways to lever an advantage.

In the BBC series *Downton Abbey*, all the servants are well aware of their responsibilities and, in some cases, jealously guard their distinction. But they show no hesitation when ferreting out any personal secrets as a power play. In fact some take great pleasure in seeing another servant publicly humiliated or embarrassed.

A young housemaid is ridiculed for taking a typing class. Her attempts to leave service are considered snobbery. Two other servants conspire to get rid of the new hire, because they resent his personal connection to the earl. Plus he guards his privacy. Upstairs is not immune either, as a rivalry between two sisters puts their family in jeopardy.

The personal mysteries are as varied as the daily menu. A few seem harmless and a little comical, while others raise ethical dilemmas. To protect his own secret, and therefore his job, a servant stands by while a daughter of the house is placed in moral danger. Later he manipulates and blackmails to attain another position before his own thievery is made public. The lure to uncover secrets for personal gain is as old as time. Cain resented God's favor of his brother's offerings over his own, and his anger resulted in murder.

Build Your Story:

1. Put your protagonist in a new workplace situation.
2. What is one thing her coworkers must not know about her?
3. How does she sidestep their questions and remain friendly?
4. Give one version where she answers with vague comments and another where she bristles at intrusion.

Doctor Who Christmas Carol

Metaphor

Often times words come out in metaphors that we need to decipher, even to ourselves. We are drawn to truths before we may know what they mean. Each of us may only glimpse pieces. So we need to share together to see the whole. Metaphors give us the creative imagination to see truth in fresh ways. And to repackage them when they've become clichés.

A Christmas Carol by Charles Dickens has become a well-worn, well-loved story that touches multiple themes. The characters themselves have become familiar echoes. It's a holiday favorite, and yet after how many times watching do we think we know the story and then discover we have forgotten key parts? Heart parts.

On a Christmas special, the Doctor Who series retold the story with familiarity and yet with differences spread throughout that kept viewers on their toes. From set design to story line, past and future merged. The streets resembled Dicken's England and yet felt odd enough to wonder what had changed, pulling you into the story immediately. For one example, the set designers had made everything out of steel riveted together. And all the windows were round or half-round. Not noticed immediately, or perhaps not at all until reading the production notes, but the effect had a metaphoric impact.

Build Your Story:

1. Take one aspect of your setting and replace a few natural parts with another texture. They may be the same color and shape but different.
2. Do one version in subtle tones and another as wildly opposite. How does it change the view?
For example: Take a main street and turn all the wooden buildings into another material, but keep the same shape. Or turn all the buildings into breathing wood.

Maps

Have you ever had a day that you would like to erase and have as a do-over? Somewhere it took control and seemingly forced you along its path with no exit signs. How can we find our way back to a new road on a fresh map?

Sometimes it seems as if our life maps are set in cement and we must follow the course we set in motion, regardless of the consequences to our emotional, physical, or spiritual health. Commitment is good. Perseverance is good. But what happens when we are so driven by agendas or choices that our route has become rigid to the point of harmful and has also left common-sense behind? Or worse, our decisions have propelled us into a skewered perspective and have twisted life out of focus.

In the *Doctor Who* version of *A Christmas Carol,* the Doctor cannot budge the hard-hearted Kazran Sardick to save a space liner. Kazran's map of bitterness has set his heart on a trajectory that he refuses to change. So the Doctor adds another set of life experiences, showing new positive memories alongside the stony ones the old man harbors. Kazran remains sarcastic and apparently unmoved, openly challenging the *Doctor's* abilities to change his mind or stop his decision to allow the crash.

But gradually he has been affected by mercy and love and grace, and when the final moment of truth comes he has changed so dramatically from himself that he is unable to reverse the controls, which will only respond to the bitter version of himself. The actions set in motion by his earlier self will not acknowledge the new. He now has a heart of truth. He must plot a new map for his life.

Build Your Story:

Take a special memory from your protagonist's past and present the original intent as opposite to her understanding. Do one from a positive reversal and one from a negative. What would change as a result in her current choices?

Memory

What makes a moment a memory? Some memories are built up over several years, such as a yearly trip to a favorite camping site, and then blend together into an image. Others are a one-time-only flash yet linger for a lifetime. And may or may not be accurate. I have a distinct memory at age five sitting on my paternal grandfather's knee in my aunt's garden as he told stories. In later years my parents insisted that it didn't happen because my grandfather had a stroke and was unable to speak. Yet it is my one and only clear memory of him. All the others remain fuzzy or based on hearsay.

Something had to have connected between us for me to hold it so thoroughly. Perhaps I was the one chattering away telling the stories, but he must have somehow engaged in the process for it to remain. Every day we have hundreds or thousands of moments that pass through our experiences unheeded. Maybe a memory sticks when, as the character says in the movie *Avatar,* "I see you."

In the *Doctor Who* series version of *A Christmas Carol,* three people experience Christmas Eve together over a period of several years. It is the only time they are together. One person ages by only one day. Another by a year. Eventually his age catches up to hers and they fall in love—for a brief few evenings. And then he discovers she has only one more time left, so rather than live it together, he lets time pass, going into his old age living off the memories and becoming more and more hard-hearted with his despair. A beautiful joy-filled adventure turned into a life of misery because he could only see it through his pain.
And when finally he opens the time again to see her vibrant expectancy, she is able to chide him softly and let her perspective enlighten his. They both "see" each other again and live the remaining moments with a connection that lasts forever.

Build Your Story:

1. Ask siblings or cousins or friends about a celebration or trip you took together as children or teens. Have them share their one highlight. Does everyone pick the same heartbeat or do a few not even remember going?

2. Repeat the exercise for your character. Then blend both sets of emotional memories into a new scene.

Mystery

Mystery opens a trail into questions. It catches us sideways with curious glimpses. When we're too busy or preoccupied to notice, it often nudges a little harder, or makes us stop a moment to consider a possibility.

In the Season Five of *Doctor Who* there is an overview story thread of a crack in the universe, (that erases memory) which then takes a backseat among all the chaos and adrenaline throughout continuing episodes. Yet in each one, following its introduction, at some point the Doctor manages to ask, "Do you remember what was in your room when we first met?"

Or suddenly he'll hesitate, look quizzical, then murmurs. "Why don't you remember?" He doesn't expect an actual answer and his companion regards him clearly confused as to why he is even asking such strange things, especially now in the middle of dire threats.

But it makes the audience remember, and we sit up, take notice, mull the possibilities, and come up with more questions. It must mean something, but what?
What does it have to do with this episode? Where's the connection? The storyline here is completely different. Or is it?
When the finale comes at season's end, we discover the intricate puzzle woven throughout and that all the pieces fit perfectly. And then I wonder how many people were prepared? And can it come back again? What other threads throughout the series will resurface?

Build Your Story:

1. Whether you've watched the series or not, make a list of causes that could create such a crack in the universe.
2. Approach it from different perspectives such as science or history, legend or architecture. Play with at least three different threads and set up cause-and-effect scenarios.

Watch with Insight

Dear Readers

Thank you for reading this workbook. Please let me know if you have any questions that didn't get covered so I can add them to this workbook or others to follow.

Also if you found this study helpful, please consider writing a review or giving a star rating on Amazon.

I hope you will drop by my blog for weekly writing prompts, conversation, and questions.

Read Deep,
Marcy

Build Your Story Blog: http://mythicimpact.blogspot.com
Website: www.marcyweydemuller.com

References and Resources

Alberts, Laurie. Showing & Telling. Cincinnati: Writer's Digest Books, Revised Edition, 2010.

Amir, Nina. How To Blog A Book. Cincinnati: Writer's Digest Books, Revised Edition, 2015.

Bell, Scott. The Art of War for Writers. Cincinnati: Writer's Digest Books, 2009.

Bourbon, Melissa, Kappes, Tonya. The Tricked-out Toolbox. Turquoise Morning Press, 2011.

Cantore, Janice. Pacific Coast Justice Series. Carol Stream: Tyndale House Publishers, Inc., 2012.

Cohen, Sage. The Productive Writer. Cincinnati: Writer's Digest Books, 2011.

Dodd, Nancy Ellen. The Writer's Compass. Cincinnati: Writer's Digest Books, 2011.

Frey, James N. The Key. New York: St. Martin's Press, 2000.

Gerke, Jeff. Plot versus Character. Cincinnati: Writer's Digest Books, Revised Edition, 2010.

George, Elizabeth. Write Away. New York: HarperCollins Publishers, 2005.

Hampl, Patricia. I Could Tell You Stories. New York: W.W. Norton & Company, Inc., 2000.

Hanley, Victoria. Wild Ink. Waco: Prufrock Press Inc., 2012.

Hughes, Monica. the Keeper of the isis Light. New York: Aladdin Paperbacks, 2000.

Ingermanson, Randy and Economy, Peter. Writing Fiction For Dummies. New Jersey: Wiley Publishing, Inc., 2010.

Kelby, N.M. The Constant Art of Being a Writer. Cincinnati: Writer's Digest Books, Revised Edition, 2009.

Nouwen, Henri J.M. The Genesee Diary. New York: Doubleday,1981.

Rosenfeld, Jordan E. Make a Scene. Cincinnati: Writer's Digest Books, 2008.

Schofield, Sandra. The Scene Book. New York: Penguin Books, 2007.

Snelling, Lauraine. A Touch of Grace. Bloomington: Bethany House Publishers, 2008.

Rebecca's Reward. Bloomington: Bethany House Publishers, 2008.

Steinbeck, John. The Log from the Sea of Cortez. New York: Penguin Books, Edition 2011.

Sundin, Sarah. On Distant Shores. Grand Rapids: Revell, 2013.

Tobias Ronald B. Theme and Strategy. Cincinnati: Writer's Digest Books, 1989.

Wiesner, Karen S. Writing the Fiction Series: The Guide for Novels and Novellas. Cincinnati: Writer's Digest Books, 2013.

Writer's Digest Editors. <u>Crafting Novels & Short Stories</u>. Cincinnati: Writer's Digest Books, 2012.

Novel Examples

Coble, Colleen. Rock Harbor Series, Hope Beach Series.

Fowler, Earlene. Bennie Harper Mystery Series.

Macias, Kathi. 12 Days of Christmas Series.

McKinlay. A Library Lover's Mystery Series.

Multiple Authors. A Pioneer Christmas Collection.

Multiple Authors. A Log Cabin Christmas Collection.

Richards, Ramona. Jackson's Retreat Series.

Movies

Avatar

A Lark Rise

Doctor Who Christmas Carol

Downton Abbey

Green Dragon

Phantom of the Opera

Secret of Moonacre

The Princess Bride

Acknowledgements

It takes a wide community to bring a project to completion, and I am very grateful for the many mentors, teachers, and authors who pave a path for each of us to follow and share their expertise through books and conferences.

For this workbook I want to give an extra-special thanks to Kitty Bucholtz, Mary Loebig Giles, Stephanie Shackelford, and Sarah Sundin for their excellent suggestions, revisions, and additional expertise.

Thank you to my family and friends who continue to encourage and sustain me with their support.

About the Author

Marcy Weydemuller lives in northern California. She is a sought-after fiction book editor, whose authors have gone on to win Writer of the Year Award at the Mount Hermon Christian Writers Conference, to final in the ACFW Genesis fiction contest finalists, and to sign multi-book contracts with publishing houses such as Revell, Beacon Hill, and Tyndale House.

She has over twenty-five years' experience writing, mentoring, and teaching fiction and nonfiction, both in person and online. She has a BA in History and Sociology, and an MFA in Writing from Vermont College of Fine Arts.

Her freelance editing services include reader feedback, developmental editing, manuscript analysis, and coaching. Projects have included historical fiction, young adult, contemporary, middle-readers—historical and contemporary, suspense-mystery, woman's romance, nonfiction, and memoir.

As an author she also writes both YA and adult fantasy, *The Lightbearers*, *Betta's Song*, historical and contemporary stories, *A Carol of Light*, *Light That Fractures*, *Invisible Light*, and has published two poetry collections, *Summer Sketches* and *Wind Sifting*. She received the 2006 Mount Hermon Poetry Award.

Write With Impact Workshop Series

Six Core Essentials For *Ongoing* Creative Inspiration

Eight Strategies For Writing *Innovative* Settings

Twelve Basic Concepts to *Influence* Your Story

Coming Soon

Four Timeless Motifs that *Power* Your Stories

Six Creative Categories to *Explore* in Journals

Eight Mythic Elements that *Add Depth* to Your Novel

www.ingramcontent.com/pod-product-compliance
Lightning Source LLC
Chambersburg PA
CBHW081626250726
48657CB00009B/2749